W0369186

HIGHLIGHT 10

Mittelschule Bayern

Workbook

für M-Klassen

Audios online verfügbar unter www.cornelsen.de/webcodes. **Code: mabawu**

Cornelsen

So viele Zeichen im Workbook – was bedeuten sie?

Die Ampel – Wie schwer fällt dir eine Übung?
In der Ampel kannst du markieren, wie schwer dir eine (Teil-)Übung gefallen ist: rot = schwer, gelb = mittel, grün = leicht.

Leere und volle Kreise – so gut du kannst
Leichtere Aufgaben sind mit einem leeren Kreis markiert und schwierigere mit einem vollen.

14

Kopfhörer – Audios online
Für diese Angebote brauchst du einen Internetzugang:
Auf *www.cornelsen.de/webcodes* findest du alle Tonaufnahmen (Audios) im MP3-Format. Der Zugangscode dafür steht auf der ersten Seite vom Workbook. Die Zahl unter dem Kopfhörer ist die Track-Nummer der Tonaufnahme.

Stift; Partnerarbeit – wie du diese Übungen bearbeiten sollst
Für Aufgaben, neben denen ein Stift abgebildet ist, schreibst du deine Antwort auf ein anderes Blatt Papier. Die Köpfe beziehen sich auf Übungen, die du zu zweit bearbeiten kannst.

I want to change the world

Unit 1

1 My place in the world

We all have connections[1] to lots of people, places and things.

- Draw circles like the ones below on a big piece of paper.
- Write these people, places and things in the right circle. Give names and examples.

family TV & film places I go hobbies school fan sites friends the environment neighbours holiday places music clubs favourite sports team pets social media friends favourite apps

Example:

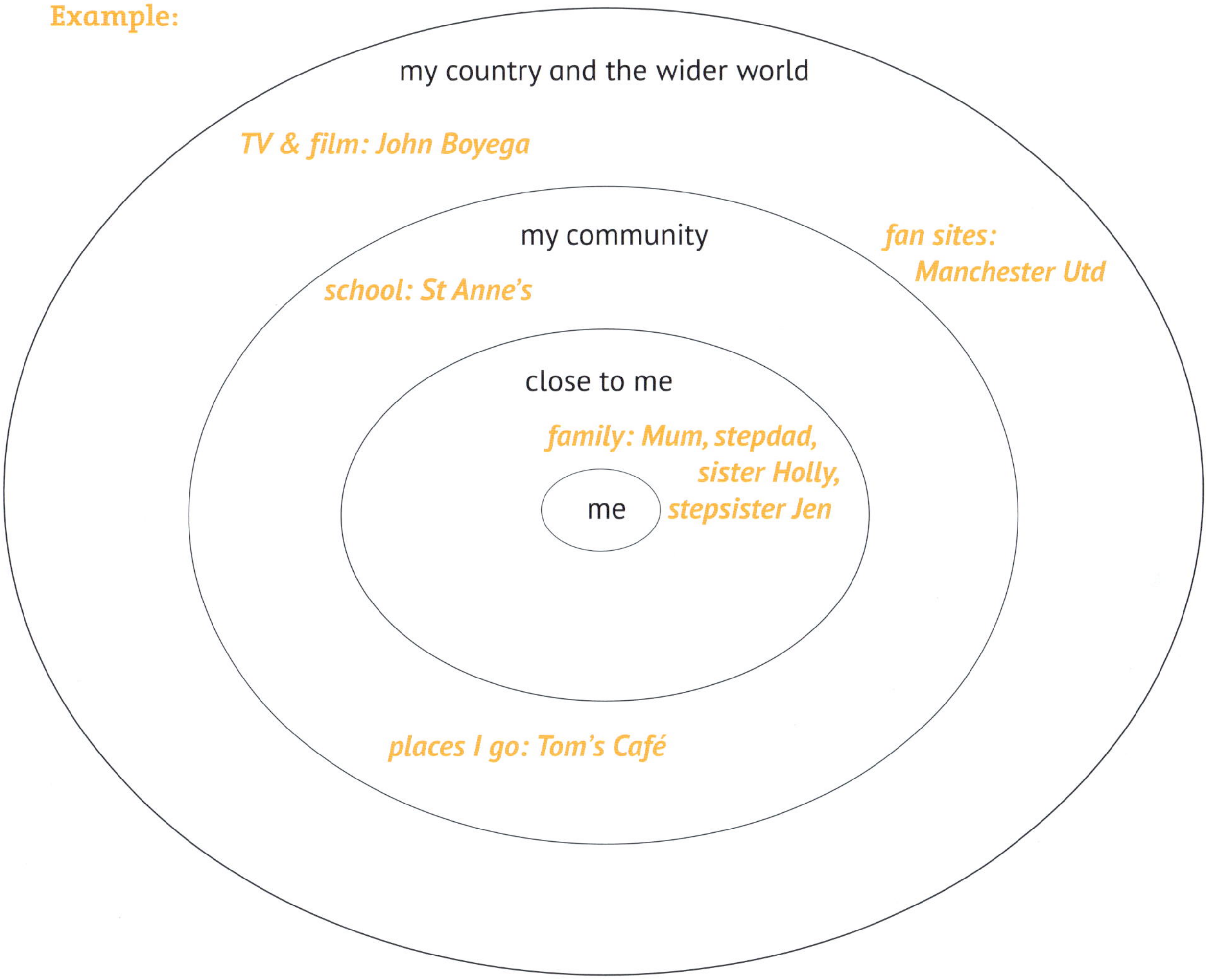

SB → p.9

2 Things I care about

Choose five things you care about and write at least three sentences about each one in your exercise book. You can choose from the ideas below, the ideas in exercise 1, or your own ideas.

animals in danger homework pocket money drugs the environment racism friends' problems violence in cities things to do in town finding a job money my future

SB → p.9

[1] connections Verbindungen

3 How can I change things?

a Complete the text with words from the box. You don't need all the words.

activists • award • campaign • create • demonstration • difference • media • petition • problems • publicize • raise • signature • volunteer

Do you feel strongly about something?

Sometimes, you have to ____________ to make the world a better place!
Here are some ways you can make a ____________.

- [ ] **1** Start an online ____________ and get people to sign it, or start one in your local area.
- [ ] **2** Add your ____________ to someone else's petition.
- [ ] **3** Be a ____________ – give some of your time to help another person or a group.
- [ ] **4** Join a group of ____________ (e.g. for the environment or human rights).
- [ ] **5** Put up posters on notice boards and in shop windows to ____________ the problem.
- [ ] **6** Talk to teachers about ____________ in your school.
- [ ] **7** Post or *like* something on social ____________ or tweet it.
- [ ] **8** Go on a ____________ with other people.
- [ ] **9** Give money, or do something to ____________ money for a charity.

b Tick (✓) the things in the list that you've already done.
Put a question mark (?) next to things you *might* do in the future.

c Discuss the things on the list with your partner. Give details.

Have you ever …
started … / signed … / been … / joined … / put up … /
talked … / posted … / been on … / given … / raised … ?

Yes, I have. No, I haven't (but I've …)
No, but one day I might.

Have you ever started a petition?

No, I haven't, but I've signed a petition about the rainforest.

d What would you like to change in society? What changes would you support?
Write two sentences.

Ideas:
rainforest / climate change / refugees / …

SB → p.11

4 Can one person change the world?
Josh is talking to his friends. He says, "I'll never be able to change the world!"
Listen to what his friends say. Write the missing words in each sentence.

1 *Tyler:* It's ______ who make a difference. They'll never ______
______.

2 *Brianna:* I would argue that ______.
One day, I want to be ______.

3 *Luis*: You can help to change some things. You can ______,
for example, or even ______.

4 *Jenna:* Online petitions ______.
I think that it's ______.
They only care ______.

5 *Hunter:* Big companies listen to ______. You can ______
______ and email them to ______.
Don't forget that small protests ______.

6 *Arianna:* All in all, there are ______
______.

SB → p.13

5 What do you think?
Do you agree or disagree with the statement "I'll never be able to change the world"? Give your arguments for or against it. Write about 60 words in your exercise book.

Useful phrases

I agree/disagree with this statement because ...
In my opinion, this statement is/isn't true because ...
I think there are good arguments for and against this statement.

On the one hand, it's true that ...
On the other hand, you can also argue that ...
An important point is that ... What's more, I would argue that ...
And besides, you should also consider that ...
Above all, ... Last but not least, ... And don't forget that ...

All in all, I think that ... To sum up, I would say that ...

TIP
You can use ideas from exercise 4 as well as your own ideas.

SB → p.13

6 Nouns and verbs

a Some words from the text (schoolbook pages 14 – 15) can be nouns *and* verbs. Find the right word in the box for each definition. You don't need all the words.

1 ____________ – *n* Einfluss; *v* beeinflussen

2 ____________ – *n* Müll; *v* bemängeln

3 ____________ – *n* Streik; *v* streiken

4 ____________ – *n* Like; *v* mögen

5 ____________ – *n* Kommentar; *v* kommentieren

6 ____________ – *n* Zweifel; *v* zweifeln

7 ____________ – *n* Behauptung; *v* behaupten

rubbish (line 1)
influence (line 6)
comment (line 26)
like (line 26)
share (line 26)
strike (lines 27, 32)
claim (line 39)
doubt (George's comments)

b Use six different words from a) in the sentences below.
- For each word, decide: Do you need noun or a verb?
- Write the word in the right form for the sentence (singular / plural; correct verb form).

1 At first, I ____________ that climate change was real, but then I realized it really was.

2 So in 2019, I joined all the *Fridays for Future* ____________.

3 When I post my opinions on social media, I get lots of interesting ____________.

4 You shouldn't ____________ environmental activists – they're trying to save the planet!

5 People say that one person can't make a difference, but Greta Thunberg has ____________ a lot of important people.

6 She doesn't make any big ____________ about being an expert, but I think she knows a lot.

SB → p.16

7 A summary

Read the section of the text: "Greta's school strike" on page 14 again. Then complete this summary.

TIP
In a summary, you give the main points only, not the details.

In 2018, Greta Thunberg was shocked by ____________________. So she started to ____________________ climate change, instead of ____________________.

Soon, she ____________ famous. Later, she decided to ____________________ only. And the ____________________ was born.

SB → p.16

FOCUS

The passive

- **Active:** Wer tut was? *People call California the Golden State.*
- **Passive:** Was wird getan? *California is called the Golden State.*
- Das Passive wird mit einer Form von (to) *be* + dem Partizip Perfekt eines Verbs gebildet.

8 San Francisco's big earthquake

Complete the article: write the verbs in the passive form (past) using the words from the boxes.

was • were

built • destroyed • felt • followed • given • ~~hit~~ • killed • made • sold

In 1906, San Francisco *was hit* ______ by a big earthquake and this ______ by a terrible fire. The earthquake ______ 560 km away in Los Angeles. Over 28,000 buildings ______ and about 3,000 people ______. Many more people ______ homeless. They ______ tents, food and water. Soon after, 5,610 wooden[1] houses ______ for people to live in. Each house cost $100-$700 to build. 100 years after the earthquake one ______ for more than $600,000!

SB → p.18

9 Hollywood

Read the article and write the verbs in the passive form (present or past).

Hollywood, Los Angeles *is known* ______ (*know*) around the world for its movies. The first Hollywood movie studio ______ (*open*) in 1911. Up to 3,000 people ______ (*employ*) to make a single film. Around 800 films ______ (*produce*) every year. 2020 was different, however: many films ______ (*delay*) because of COVID-19, and a lot of money ______ (*lose*). The famous Hollywood sign ______ (*visit*) by over 10 million people each year. It ______ (*put up*) in 1923 as an advert for new houses, but people liked it, so it ______ (*leave*)! Now, it ______ (*love*) by people around the world!

SB → p.18

[1] wooden Holz, aus Holz

FOCUS

The past perfect

- Wenn zwei Handlungen in der Vergangenheit passieren, verwendest du das Past Perfekt für die Handlung, die *vor* der zweiten Handlung passierte.

  We had booked rooms at a hostel before we started our road trip.
  We went to the beach after we had been to the hostel to check in.

- Das *past perfekt* wird mit had und dem Partizip Perfekt gebildet.

10 Before Rosalia arrived

What had Diego and his mom done before Rosalia's visit? Write sentences with the past perfect.

Diego: invite friends to a welcome party ✓ make a cake ✓ get the tent out of the garage ✓
Mom: plan a road trip ✓ book tickets for a film studio ✓ clean the house ✓

Diego had ______________________________

He had also ______________________________

And he ______________________________

His mom had ______________________________

She ______________________________

And she ______________________________

SB → p.20

11 After Rosalia had left

Read Diego's email to Rosalia. Write the verbs in the simple past and the past perfect.

TIP

Negatives simple past: I didn't do …
past perfect: I hadn't done …

After you ____________ *(return)* home, I was bored. I ____________ *(want)* to go out with my friends but Mom ____________ *(say)* no, because I ____________ *(not do)* my homework. So I ____________ *(do)* my homework. Then Mom ____________ *(tell)* me I couldn't go out because I ____________ *(not tidy)* my room. After I ____________ *(put)* all my things away, I ____________ *(shout)* downstairs to Mom. She ____________ *(not answer)* – she ____________ *(go out)*! She ____________ *(leave)* a note on the table: "Please do the shopping – here's a list". I couldn't believe it!

SB → p.20

12 SPEAKING Picture-based conversation

PARTNER A *(Partner B: Go to page 47)*

a Look at the two pictures below for about 30 seconds.
Then answer Partner A's questions. Talk for three minutes.

Travelling Picture 1

Travelling Picture 2

Useful phrases

Differences:	Picture A **shows people who** are ...ing.
	On the other hand, picture B **shows** ...
Similarities:	In **both** pictures ...
Mood:	In picture A, the people **look** (relaxed / happy, ...)
How they're interacting:	The people are... talking to **each other** / laughing **together** / ...

b Look at Partner B's pictures. Ask two questions from Set A and three questions from Set B.

Set A
- Describe the differences in the pictures.
- Describe the similarities[1] in the pictures.
- Give a detailed description of what the people are doing in the first picture / second picture.
- What is the general mood of the pictures?
- How are the people in each picture interacting[2] with each other?

Set B
- What do you think about people who leave rubbish? Why?
- What do you and your family buy that creates a lot of rubbish?
- What are other problems for the environment?
- What other types of volunteering can people do (not just for the environment)?

SB → p. 21

[1] similarity Ähnlichkeit [2] interact aufeinander wirken

03 **13 LISTENING Preparing for a trip abroad**

Grace is planning a trip abroad. She goes to the bank. Listen and write short answers.

TIP

Remember: *write short answers* means you don't have to write sentences.

1 What information is Grace looking for?

___

2 Which countries is she going to visit?

___

3 How can she get money in India?

___

4 How much money does Grace change *in total*? ___

5 What must Grace show the man? ___

6 What does the man tell her *not* to do, and why?

don't ___

because ___

SB → p.23

14 WRITING Express[1] your own ideas: volunteering abroad

Answer this question and give three reasons. Write at least 60 words.

Would you like to do volunteer work abroad one day?

Show how good your English is! Use complex phrases and sentences, e.g. I'd **really** like to / I **probably** wouldn't like to ... **because** ...
If you're a volunteer, you **can**...
On the one hand, ... **On the other hand**, ...
I think it would **certainly** be... **However**, ...

Some ideas:
exciting • experience
hard work • local
communities • miss my
friends • team
traditional homestay

___

___

___

___

___

___

SB → p.23

[1] express ausdrücken

15 Opposites

Write the opposites of these words, by adding: im- / in- / un-.

1 happy ________ 4 friendly ________ 7 healthy ________

2 able ________ 5 possible ________ 8 dependent ________

3 polite ________ 6 equality ________ 9 comfortable ________

SB → p.25

16 Useful phrases

a Complete the dialogue with the phrases from the box. There's one extra.

I have my doubts about • it's no use • it's worth • last but not least • put up with • take advantage of • used to

Luis: I'm fed up with people complaining about climate change but doing nothing about it. ________ just talking about it – you have to do something! We shouldn't ________ politicians who don't take action. Society can change: years ago, we ________ put all our rubbish in the same bin, but now we recycle.

Jenna: I don't know. ________ how much one person can do ...

Luis: But you don't have to do things alone! I really believe ________ joining a campaign, going on a demonstration, signing a petition and – ________ ________ – just talking to other people about things you care about.

b Now use the phrases from a) to write the phrases in **red** in a different way. Make any changes you need to.

Jenna: School is so boring now! A few years ago, (we had) *we* ________ lots of clubs.

Luis: (We shouldn't just complain) *It's* ________ about it. We shouldn't (accept) ________ a boring school. (We should ask) ________ ________ the principal if we could have some clubs.

Jenna: (I'm not sure about) ________ that. She won't listen to us.

Luis: We'll give good reasons: first, clubs will be good for students' education; second, they'll be good for our mental health and, (finally) ________, parents will like the idea.

SB → p.25

Das kann ich auf Englisch!
Hier kannst du überprüfen, ob und wie gut du alles verstanden hast. Finde auch heraus, wo du dich noch verbessern kannst. Was kannst du schon sehr gut ● oder recht gut ●? Was musst du noch üben ●? Male die Ampellichter entsprechend aus.

1 Ich kann meine Haltung zu einem bestimmten Sachverhalt darlegen und begründen.
- Put the words in the right order to make phrases to agree or disagree.

WB → S.5, Nr.4–5

1 hand, / the / on / one / ... ______

2 with / I / this / disagree / statement. ______

3 up, / to / would / I / say / sum / ... ______

4 all / all, / think / I / in / that / ... ______

2 Ich kann sagen, was mit einer Person oder Sache getan wird oder getan wurde.
- Complete the sentences with the right form of the passive: past or present.

WB → S.7, Nr.8–9

In the summer of 2021, some parts of Germany ______ *(hit)* by terrible floods. Lots of houses ______ *(wash)* away and hundreds of people ______ *(injured)* or lost their lives and many more people ______ *(make)* homeless. Now communities are trying to make plans so that their towns ______ *(protect)* from future weather catastrophes.

3 Ich kann mich bei der Bank über Zahlungsmöglichkeiten bei einem Auslandsaufenthalt informieren.
- Complete the sentences with the right words from the box. One word is extra.
- Who says it? Write B for bank clerk and C for customer.

WB → S.10, Nr. 13

exchange rates • ATM • prepaid • passport • change • information

____ 1 I need some cash. Could you tell me where the nearest ______ is please?

____ 2 I need some ______ about the best way to take money abroad.

____ 3 Please could you show me your ______?

____ 4 You could buy a ______ travel card before you go.

____ 5 The ______ are better at the bank. You should change money there.

FOCUS

The simple past and past progressive

- Das **simple past** beschreibt, was in der Vergangenheit geschehen ist oder was jemand getan hat; die Handlung/das Ereignis ist abgeschlossen. *Yesterday I went to the cinema.*
- Mit dem **past progressive** drückst du aus, dass etwas zu einer bestimmten Zeit in der Vergangenheit im Gang (noch nicht abgeschlossen) war. *While I was watching the film, my phone rang.*

You might use these tenses in a story in the exam.

1 Drama at the coast

a Write the verbs in the simple past or past progressive.

TIPP

Impress the examiner[1]: don't just use the simple past – use the past progressive too!

Last weekend, Kara and Ruben (not stay) ____________ at home – they (go) ____________ to the coast. It (rain) ____________ heavily when they (arrive) ____________, so they (not get out) ____________ of the car.

While they (have) ____________ lunch, Kara (notice) ____________ a boy in the sea. He (not move) ____________. They (not wait) ____________ another minute – Ruben (phone) ____________ the emergency services. While he (do) ____________ that, Kara (run) ____________ into the sea. When she (bring) ____________ the boy out of the water, he (not breathe) ____________, so Ruben (give) ____________ him CPR[2].

Soon, the boy (start) ____________ to breathe again. When the ambulance (come) ____________, the boy (already sit) ____________ in the car.

b How does the story end? Write two or three sentences.

Ideas: paramedic[3] / boy / ... say well done! / do the right thing / save my life / ...

____

____

[1] examiner Person, die prüft [2] CPR Herz-Lungen-Wiederbelebung [3] paramedic Sanitäter / Sanitäterin

Unit 2

English at work

1 Using English at work

04 a Listen to two people who use English at work. Fill in the gaps with 1–4 words.

Jonas works as a ______________________________

in the centre of Regensburg.

People go there from ______________________________.

Jonas speaks English when the guests ______________________,

and if they have any questions or problems. He often uses English

__________________________. It's useful for __________________ too.

Jasmin works in the ______________________________

of a large firm in Munich.

She sometimes uses English when she needs to find

______________________________.

Some important customers go to her office __________________________. These sometimes take place in English. And when they go __________________________ in the evening they talk in English. Jasmin often has to __________________________ for English speaking countries.

b Why do you want / need to learn English? Talk to a partner.

SB → p. 27

2 A Welsh[1] marketing trick

You find this interesting article. Make notes in German for a friend who doesn't speak English.

TIP

How do Welsh people say this name? You can find videos online. Put "How to say Llanfair PG" into a search engine[2].

Llanfairpwllgwyngyllgogerychwyrndrobwllllantysiliogogogoch
(or Llanfair PG for short!) is a village in North Wales, where a lot of people speak Welsh as well as English. It has the longest place name in Europe! Its name was made longer in the 19th century as a marketing trick to bring tourists – and it worked: around 200,000 visitors come every year. The most popular thing there is the very long sign at the railway station!

SB → p. 27

[1] Welsh walisisch [2] search engine Suchmaschine

3 Problems with an order

Filip has some problems with ordering equipment for their office.
Complete this email with words from the box. There are two extra words.

afraid • attached • confirm • damaged • delivered • exchange • faithfully • hearing • let • make • packaging • receive • replacement • return • Sir

Dear ______________ / Madam

Our order of office equipment was ______________ today (order No. RN73139), but I'm ______________ that there are some problems with it. The desk lamp is ______________ (see the ______________ photo). Could you please send a ______________? Unfortunately, the five floor mats we ordered are too big, so we would like to ______________ them. Can you please ______________ that you have five mats in the smaller size? Please ______________ us know how to ______________ the lamp and the mats. We still have the ______________.

I look forward to ______________ from you.

Yours ______________
Filip Nowak

SB → p. 28

4 Customers on the phone

Listen to these phone calls to Black's, an office equipment company.
■ Why is each customer phoning? ◆ What answer do they get? Write short answers.

1 ■ *display stand is* ______________
◆ *they'll* ______________

2 ■ ______________
◆ ______________

3 ■ ______________
◆ ______________

4 ■ ______________
◆ ______________

SB → p. 28

5 Describing people

a Read what these people say. Which adjective describes each person? There's one extra.

careful • confident • flexible • polite • punctual • reliable • rude • tidy • unhelpful

1. I'm never late for a meeting. I always arrive 10 minutes early. ______
2. You can't come today? No problem. Thursday or Friday is fine instead. ______
3. No, I haven't forgotten about the meeting later. If I say I'll be there, I *will* be there! ______
4. I don't like your hair. It looks terrible! And your new shirt is horrible too. ______
5. Could I borrow your pen, please? Would you mind? ... Oh, thank you very much. ______
6. I can speak French well. When I go to Paris, I'll be OK. ______
7. You're finding the work difficult? Well, I don't have time to show you how to do it... ______
8. I always think about what I'm writing, and I check my work. I don't want to make mistakes. ______

b Which adjectives describe you best? Write sentences.

I'm very / quite / usually / often / sometimes ...

SB → p. 30

6 What job is it?

a Choose five jobs from the list below. Describe what you think is important for each job – but don't write the name of the job! Write in your exercise book.

Example: *To be a ______ you need to be friendly, helpful and patient and have good communication skills. You have to be good with young people. You need to be able to organize yourself. And you should be good at maths!*

TIP
You can find useful words and phrases on pages 30–31 of your schoolbook.

marketing trainee • waiter / waitress • doctor • police officer • web designer • singer • fashion designer • receptionist • cook • farmer • sports coach • mechanic • care worker • taxi driver • tour guide

b Your partner reads your descriptions and writes the names of the jobs.

Example: *To be a* ______ *you need to be ...*

SB → p.31

7 New words puzzle

Complete the crossword with new words from the text on pages 32–33 in your schoolbook.

Across →
1 Look through pages (on a phone) = (...) through pages
3 The presentation went well. She didn't (...) up.
5 our newest products = our (...) products
8 I didn't stop practising. = I (...) practising.
10 Talking to (...) people is easier than talking to a crowd.
11 "You want *me* to give a presentation?! (...) way!"

Down ↓
2 We thought of a plan. = We (...) up with a plan.
4 She had a confident (...) on her face.
5 She went into the bathroom and (...) the door.
6 believe in someone = never give (...) on someone
7 concentrate on something = (...) on something
9 go through someone's mind quickly = (...) through someone's mind

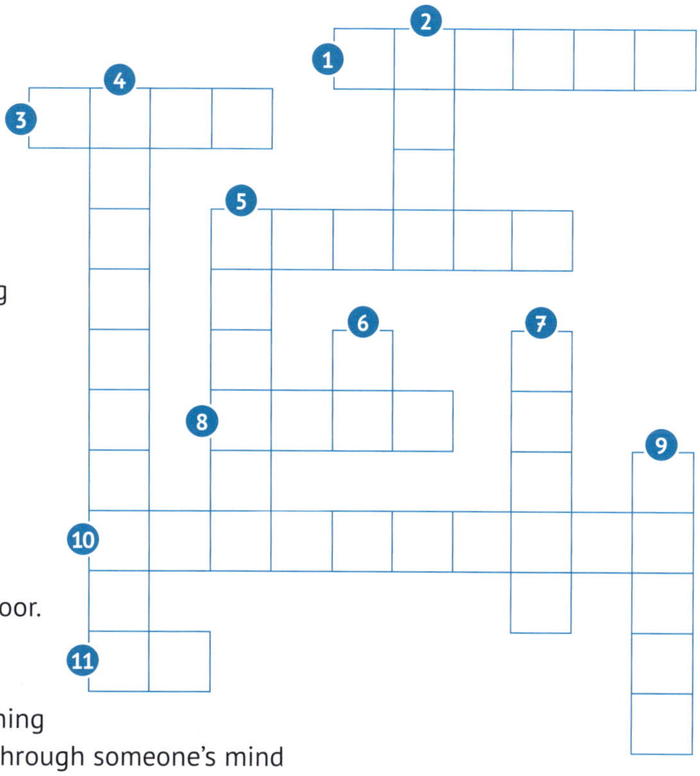

SB → p.34

8 Giving a presentation

a You find this article about giving a presentation and want to make notes for yourself.
- First, **highlight** key ideas in the text.
- Write the ideas as a list of tips in your exercise book.

TIP
You can change the words in the article to make your list short and simple.

There are lots of ways you can make sure your presentation is a success. Begin by planning it carefully. You'll need to decide on the different aspects you'll talk about. That's the first thing. Don't forget to think about who your target audience is. Having notes that are easy to read will be very helpful. Nice pictures can make your presentation more interesting.

You'll find that practising your presentation can help you to feel confident. While you practise, listen to your voice: does it sound boring? You don't want that!

When you begin your presentation, try to relax. Speaking loudly and clearly is very important, so that everyone can hear you well. People who are nervous often speak too quickly, and it can be hard for people to understand. And last but not least, don't forget to smile. You'll look and feel more confident!

b Prepare and give a short presentation to a group of three other students. Use your list of tips to help you.
You'll find some useful phrases on page 64.

You can choose any subject you like, e.g. a hobby, a pet, a place you love.

SB → p. 34

FOCUS

Word order

- Aussagesätze: **Subject** – **Verb** – **Object**
  At first *I* *didn't know* *Tom* *very well.*
  But soon *we* *became* *good friends.*
- Fragen: *did/do* kommt vor dem Subjekt: *When* ***did*** ***you*** ***meet*** *Tom?*
- **Ort** vor Zeit *I met Tom at a friend's house three months ago.*

9 Correct the mistakes

A student has made some mistakes. Some words are in the wrong place. Please help!

- Underline the mistakes and draw arrows (→) to show where the words *should* be.
- Then write the sentences correctly.

1 We went in August to North Wales.

____

2 I loved it because the countryside very beautiful is.

____

3 We have a cousin who there lives.

____

4 At first stayed we with our cousin.

____

5 I thought that his house very nice was.

____

6 We didn't know very well the area.

____

7 It was fun to visit every day new places.

____

8 What did you in the summer holidays do?

____

SB → p. 36

FOCUS

Indirect speech

- Bei indirekter Rede wird **das Verb** meist um eine Zeitstufe in die Vergangenheit „zurückverschoben".
- Das **Pronomen** wird geändert: z.B. I → she
- Bei Aussagesätzen verwendest du *that*. Bei Fragen verwendest du *if*.

Direkte Rede (direct speech)	Indirekte Rede (indirect speech)
*Amira: "**I'm** happy to see **you**, Tom."*	*Tom: Amira said **that she was** happy to see **me**.*
*"**I've brought** an invitation."*	*She said **that she had brought** an invitation.*
*"**Do you like** parties?"*	*She asked **if I liked** parties.*

10 Amy's ex-boyfriend

Amy tells her friend Eliana about her ex-boyfriend, Sam. Change the words in blue and complete what Amy said to Eliana.

Amy's conversation with Sam	What Amy told Eliana

	Sam was OK, but after six weeks we argued...
1 Amy: Do you like cats?	1 I asked *if he* ________ cats.
2 Sam: I hate your cat.	2 He said *that* ________ *my* ________ cat!
3 Amy: Well your dog smells horrible!	3 So I told him *that* ________ dog ________ horrible.
4 Sam: And your friends are boring.	4 And then he said ________ friends ________ boring.
5 Amy: I've never liked your friends!	5 So I said ________ never ________ friends!
6 Sam: Good! Because they aren't going to come to your party!	6 He said ________ come to ________ party.
7 Amy: Well, I haven't invited them!	7 I said ________ them.
8 Sam: Do you think I care about that?	8 He asked *I* ________ *he* ________ about that.
9 Sam: I never want to see you again!	9 He said ________ never ________ to see ________ again!
10 Amy: Well, I'm happy with that!	10 So I told him ________ happy with that!

SB → p.38

Visit Machynlleth

Introducing Machynlleth

Machynlleth is a Welsh market town with a long history. Situated in the west of Wales, Machynlleth lies about 17 km from the coast. But how on earth do you pronounce the town's typical Welsh name?! Well, the 'ch' is like German *Bach*; 'yn' sounds like 'un'; and to say 'll' – whisper 'l' loudly! Local people call it 'Mach' for short.

The annual comedy festival

Each year, on the first weekend in May, Machynlleth's small population of about 2,500 welcomes about 8,000 comedy fans from all over the UK and beyond for its comedy festival. The festival includes some of the UK's top comedians as well as those who are less famous. There are hundreds of great comedy shows, which are held in different venues, small and larger, in the town centre. The prices aren't expensive, and you can buy tickets for the shows when you get to Machynlleth, but some sell out quickly, so if you don't want to be disappointed, book online before you go.

Accommodation is available in and around Machynlleth – B&Bs and holiday cottages – and the festival also has its own campsite. But don't wait till the last minute to arrange your accommodation, because they soon get full! You can buy a range of good quality street food at the festival, and the town itself has a good number of cafés, pubs and restaurants.

Comedy is the main focus of the festival, but the Beech Bar has free music all weekend and there are also free things for families in the kids' tent.

The Centre for Alternative Technology

5 km north of Machynlleth is the Centre for Alternative Technology (CAT), an eco-centre with a focus on sustainable living. It has an eco-house, organic gardens and an exhibition centre with interactive family-friendly displays.

But it isn't just a centre where ordinary visitors can learn how to do more for the environment in their own homes. It also has short and long training courses on environmental topics for industry professionals. CAT also does its own research: it studies new ways to fight climate change.

So, CAT does some very serious work ... But don't be fooled – a family visit to CAT is lots of fun! There are great activities for kids of all ages, and fantastic places to play in the woods around the centre.

You can buy tickets for CAT at the centre itself or on the website. CAT has a gift shop and a great café with a fully vegetarian and vegan menu, including salads and vegetables from the centre's own vegetable garden.

11 READING A great place to visit

Morgan works in a tourist office in Wales. He's made a web page about the town of Machynlleth. Read the text and write the line number(s) where you find the following information.

1 Machynlleth is an old town.	line ______
2 Thousands of people go to the comedy festival there.	line ______
3 Tickets for the festival don't cost a lot.	line ______
4 It's best to book early if you need somewhere to stay.	line ______
5 People can study environmental issues seriously at CAT.	line ______
6 At CAT, they grow some of their own food.	line ______

SB → p.40

12 MEDIATION Visit Machynlleth

Your friend has seen the web page but doesn't speak English very well. Answer his questions in German.

1 Wo liegt Machynlleth und wie groß ist die Stadt?

______

______

2 Welche Angebote bietet das *Centre for Alternative Technology* für Kinder und Familien?

______

______

3 Wo kann ich übernachten, wenn ich das Comedy Festival besuchen möchte?

______

______

4 Wofür muss ich auf dem Comedy Festival bezahlen und gibt es auch kostenlose Aktionen?

______

______

5 Wie kann ich Karten für das CAT und die Comedy-Shows erhalten?

______

______

SB → p.40

13 A weekend job

Read this text by Lucy from Machynlleth. Write the words in brackets in the correct form.

I have a new weekend job. I'm ________________ (interest) in history, and I do ________________ (guide) tours of the town. I ________________ (do) about 10 tours already. When I started the job, I ________________ (give) some training by the tourist office, ________________ (who) manager was very ________________ (help). Lots of ________________ (visit) come in the summer, ________________ (special) for the comedy festival, which has some of the ________________ (good) comedians. These top ________________ (perform) come from all over the UK.

TIP

Sometimes you need more than one word. *play* → *have played.*

SB → p. 42

14 Fun with words

In this word game you have to find as many words as possible with letters from another word.

* The words can be two letters or longer.
* You can only use each letter once (unless[1] the original word has more than one).

Here's an example:

Festival

sit	*fit*	*is*	*leaf*	*eat*
sat	*felt*	*it*	*late*	*eats*
save	*fail*	*itself*	*live*	
sale	*flat*		*lives*	
salt	*false*		*list*	*as*
	five	*tail*	*last*	*at*
		tails		*ate*

TIP

- Write your words in lists starting with the same letter.
- Think of letters that go together, e.g. 'ai', 'ea', 'ch', 'th'.

Now you! How many words can you find in the words 'COMEDIAN' or 'MACHYNLLETH'?

COMEDIAN

Scores:
4–6 – not bad
7–9 – very good
10–13 – brilliant!
14–20+ – totally amazing!

Compare words with a partner. What score do you get together?

MACHYNNLLETH

Scores:
8–14 – not bad
15–22 – very good
23–30 – brilliant!
31–40+ – totally amazing!

SB → p. 43

[1] unless – es sei denn

Das kann ich auf Englisch!
Hier kannst du überprüfen, ob und wie gut du alles verstanden hast. Finde auch heraus, wo du dich noch verbessern kannst. Was kannst du schon sehr gut ● oder recht gut ●? Was musst du noch üben ● ? Male die Ampellichter entsprechend aus.

1 Ich kann eine formale E-Mail schreiben.

- Match the beginnings of the sentences to the ends. WB → S.15, Nr.3

1 I'm afraid
2 Please let us know when
3 Please can you confirm
4 I look forward
5 Unfortunately, the equipment

a you can send a replacement.
b to hearing from you.
c there is a problem with our order.
d was not delivered on time.
e that you have received my email?

2 Ich kann sprachliche Regelmäßigkeiten erkennen.

- Put the words in the right order to make a correct question and two correct sentences. WB → S.18, Nr.9

1 **How much time** ... spend / phone / do / on / your / you?

____

2 **Amir doesn't use his phone in class because** ... doesn't / it / his / teacher / allow.

____

3 **No one believes me when** ... tell / phone / don't have / I / I / them / a.

____

3 Ich kann berichten, was jemand gesagt hat.

- You meet your friend Leila on the street. Tell your dad what Leila said. Put her words into indirect speech. WB → S.19, Nr.10

Leila said, „It's good to see you! How are you? I'm going on holiday tomorrow. I'll call you when I get back."

Leila said that it was _______________

____

____

____

FOCUS

The simple past and present perfect

- Das **simple past** beschreibt, was in der Vergangenheit geschehen ist oder was jemand getan hat; die Handlung/das Ereignis ist abgeschlossen. *Yesterday I went to the cinema.*
- Mit dem **present perfect** drückst du aus, dass etwas in der Vergangenheit begonnen hat und jetzt noch andauert, oder dass du etwas schon einmal, oft oder nie gemacht hast. *I've never worked in a hotel.*

You might use these tenses in an email or letter about yourself in the exam.

TIP

Remember: If a *specific time* is given, use the simple past. *Yesterday* I went…

1 Application for a summer job

a Read part of Elena's letter. Underline the signal words / phrases – in pencil for the ones you need the simple past for and in pen for the present perfect.

b Circle the correct forms of the verbs: simple past or present perfect.

I am writing to apply for a summer job at your campsite, where I've stayed / I stayed with my parents last April. We all enjoyed / We've all enjoyed our holiday with you. Although I didn't work / I haven't worked at a campsite before, I've had / I had lots of experience of customer service. For example, two years ago I've helped / I helped in my uncle's shop, and last summer I had / I've had a job at a cafe. I've been camping / I went camping lots of times with my family, so I understand what your customers need.

TIP

go → I *went* to London. / I*'ve been* to London.

2 A job application

Albie wants to work in a clothes shop in Liverpool. Write some of the sentences he needs. Use the simple past or present perfect.

1 already work – in two clothes shops
2 last month – do – a customer service training course
3 although – never visit Liverpool – go to the UK five times
4 in last job – win – 'salesperson of the year'

1 ______________________________

2 ______________________________

____

3 ______________________________

4 ______________________________

Respect for all!

Unit 3

1 Respect other people!

a Listen to two people discussing one of the pictures below. Complete the sentences.

1 They're talking about picture **A B C D.** (Circle the correct letter.)

2 They think the waiter should ______________________.

3 The man uses a wheelchair, but that doesn't mean ______________________.

4 Not speaking to the man directly will ______________________.

A

B

C

D

b Look at the other pictures and make some notes in your exercise book.

- What's happening in the picture?
- Some of the people aren't showing respect. What are they doing?
- What should they do? What shouldn't they do? Why?

You shouldn't / It's wrong to...	be rude / be unkind / ...
It'll hurt their feelings.	It isn't fair / nice / ...
It'll make (the man) feel...	It'll make the park look ...
You should... show respect / think about other people / be patient / ...	

c Close your exercise book. Discuss all four pictures with a partner. Do you agree?

d Have you seen or experienced a situation where someone didn't show respect? What happened? What did you think about it? Talk to your partner or write in your exercise book.

SB → p.45

2 Talking about the generation gap

You've met a British girl, Leah. Your friend Emil wants to talk to her, but he doesn't speak good English. Interpret[1] what they say.

- If you don't understand an English word when you're interpreting into German, you can ask what it means.
- If you don't know the English word or phrase you need, find another way of saying the same thing:

e.g. *"Ich bin mir nicht sicher."* => you can say

"I don't know exactly." (instead of "I'm not sure.").

Emil: Findest du, dass es einen Generationenkonflikt zwischen dir und deinen Eltern gibt?

You: ______

Leah: Sometimes. I think they don't realize that the world has changed since they were young!

You: ______

______

Emil: Meine Eltern finden, dass ich zu viel Zeit mit meinem Handy verbringe. Sie verstehen das nicht.

You: ______

Leah: I try to help my parents to see things from my point of view.

You: ______

______

Emil: Es ist wichtig, sich gegenseitig zu respektieren.

You: *(Du kennst das Wort 'gegenseitig' nicht auf Englisch. Sag es mit anderen Worten.)*

______

______

Leah: Sometimes I don't agree with my parents at first, but then I see that they're right!

You: ______

______

Emil: Ja, ich glaube, es lohnt sich, ihnen zuzuhören.

You: ______

SB → p.46

[1] interpret dolmetschen

3 Advice about cyberbullying

a Read the advice and fill the gaps with words from the box. You won't need all the words.

answer • anxiety • definitely • evidence • negative • one in three • opportunity • otherwise • persuade • problem • promote • realise • say • target • tell • whether

Over ______________ people today feel that they've experienced cyberbullying at some time in their life. That's a lot! Being bullied can make you feel helpless, and maybe you hope it will just stop – but ______________ you want to or not, you need to do something about it! ______________, it might go on and on and make you feel worse, and also the bully might ______________ other people too. So what can you do?

- If you're a victim of bullying, don't feel alone. You should ______________ tell an adult you trust. They can help you make the ______________ go away.
- If you get horrible messages, comments or emails, don't ______________ them. But take a screenshot or keep them as ______________ to show to an adult.
- If it's on social media, ______________ the website you're being bullied. Many people don't ______________ that you can do this safely and easily. And obviously, you can block the bully.
- A bully might try to ______________ you that the bullying is somehow *your* fault. That's not true. Remember – it's really the bully who has a problem. Perhaps they're jealous or want to hide something ______________ in their own life.

b A website about bullying says: 'If you're feeling unhappy, do positive things that make you feel good.' Write five or more things that can make someone feel good.

Listen to your favourite ... ______________

____

____

SB → p.49

4 Racism or respect
Look again at the text on pages 50–51 in your schoolbook.

a Which sentence is a good summary of Seretse and Ruth's story: A, B or C? ___

A Seretse and Ruth didn't care what other people thought about their inter-racial marriage – they just wanted a happy family.

B Racist people hated their inter-racial marriage, but Seretse and Ruth showed that respect for others is better for everyone.

C A racist government will always fall in the end because it isn't fair.

b Read this longer summary of the first part of the text (lines 1–58). Complete the sentences with the right verbs.

Verbs:

accepted	improve	~~married~~	sold
banned	invited	needed	surprised
didn't want	judged	refused to	used
had met	led	showed	weren't

Seretse Khama and Ruth Williams, 1965

The text is about a black man, Seretse Khama, and a white woman, Ruth Williams, who married ______ in 1948. They ______ at a dance. Seretse was the son of an African king.

Seretse's people ______ accept a white woman as queen, but Ruth ______ them respect and they ______ her. This ______ everybody.

But Ruth and Seretse's problems ______ over. South Africa's racist government ______ a happy inter-racial marriage in a neighbouring country. Britain, who ______ South Africa's gold, ______ Seretse to London, then ______ him from returning to Botswana as king.

But Seretse triumphed: he ______ Botswana to independence and was its first president. You can see the story in the film *A United Kingdom*. Botswana was very poor, so Seretse ______ money from selling diamonds to ______ life for his people.

c Make the summary better! Each paragraph in b) has one sentence that isn't needed. Decide which sentence and draw a line through it. Then compare with your partner.

A good summary only has the *most important and relevant* points.

SB → p.52

FOCUS

Conditional sentences Type II

- Hiermit sagst du, was unter bestimmten Bedingungen geschehen würde.
- Das Verb im if-Satz steht im **simple past**; das Verb im Hauptsatz enthält would ('d) + Infinitiv
  If I had enough money, I'd visit Australia.
  My mum would go to the USA if the flight wasn't so long.

5 Holiday dreams ...

18-year-old Mohammed is dreaming of a great holiday when he leaves school in the summer. Complete his sentences with the right forms of the verbs.

Remember: If I ***had*** ...
NOT If I ~~*would have*~~ ...

If I __________ (have) enough money, I __________ (go) travelling round Australia. If my friend Riley __________ (come) with me, we __________ (have) an awesome time! We __________ (be able to) see lots of different places if we __________ (spend) the whole summer there. But a big trip like that __________ (be) expensive – I __________ (not be able to) afford it. If I __________ (get) a summer job, maybe I __________ (earn) enough money... But probably not! Of course, if I __________ (work) all summer, I __________ (not have) time for a long holiday! But if I __________ (not earn) any money, there __________ (be) no holiday at all for me! Hmm... I need a better plan!

SB → p.54

6 What would you do ... ?

a Write these questions in your exercise book and then write your own answers. Put the verbs in the right form.

What would you do...

1. ... if you (win) a trip to any country in the world?
2. ... if you (find) 200 euros in the street?
3. ... if you (see) a ghost?
4. ... if you (not have to) go to school any more?
5. ... if you (meet) your favourite star?
6. ... if you (can) choose a magic power?

I'd probably choose the power to be invisible[1]!

b Ask lots of people in your class the same questions. Can you find someone who gives an answer that's the same or similar to yours for each question?

SB → p.54

[1] invisible unsichtbar

FOCUS

The present perfect progressive and the present perfect

- Das **present perfect progressive** verwendest du, wenn du ausdrücken willst, dass etwas in der Vergangenheit begonnen hat und bis (oder fast bis) zum Zeitpunkt des Sprechens andauert. Die Handlung und ihre Dauer stehen im Vordergrund. **Es wird mit** have/has + been + der ing-Form des Verbs **gebildet**.
- Das **present perfect** verwendest du, wenn du ausdrücken willst, dass etwas vor dem Zeitpunkt des Sprechens geschehen ist. Hier steht das Ergebnis der Handlung im Vordergrund. **Es wird mit** have/has + dem Partizip Perfekt **gebildet**.

7 Social media ... and real life!

a Joanna is on holiday. Read her social media post and circle the correct forms of the verbs: **present perfect progressive, past perfect** or **simple past**.

I'm so lucky to be in Jaipur, in the north of India! I've never visited / I've never been visiting India before – it's awesome! We've been staying / We've stayed in Jaipur since Monday. We've already seen / We've already been seeing the beautiful southern state of Kerala.

The food here in India is fantastic – we ate / we've been eating lots of wonderful curries! Last week it was / it has been the Diwali holiday – the festival of lights. It was amazing! And this week here in Jaipur we've been visiting / we visited lots of awesome palaces and temples. I took / I've been taking lots of photos every day – here are a few.

24 6 comments

b But what's the holiday *really* like? Read Joanna's email to her friend. Write the nine verbs in the correct form. You'll need the present perfect progressive six times, and two other tenses.

I ______________ (have) a good time here, but my sister ______________ (annoy) me a lot. She ______________ (use) my things without asking me, so we ______________ (argue) every day. Mum ______________ (complain) about the heat – well, what did she expect when she ______________ (book) a holiday to India?! And curry's nice, but I ______________ (dream) of fish and chips! When I get home, that's the first thing I ______________ (eat)!

SB → p.56

8 READING Respect others when you travel

a Six sentences are missing in the article below.
Read the sentences (A-H) and match them with the gaps (1-6).
There are two extra sentences.

> Read carefully what comes *before* the gap – and *after* it!

Travelling to other countries is a great way to see new places and learn about other cultures. __(1)__ Going to someone else's country is like going to their house – you need to be polite and respectful!

It's a good idea to find out a little about the culture of the country before your holiday, especially if its culture is very different from your own. You can find information about a country's habits[1] and traditions online and in travel guides. __(2)__

For example, if you're going to visit a church or temple, think about what clothes you should wear. __(3)__ So in many places it wouldn't be respectful to wear the same clothes that you'd wear on a beach. Check to see if you should wear something over your legs and on your head.

What other customs does the country have? Should you shake hands if you're introduced to someone? Should you give a tip[2] to waiters and taxi drivers? __(4)__

Of course, you won't be able to speak the language of every country you visit. But it helps to learn a few useful words and phrases, like *hello, goodbye, please* and *thank you*. People will be pleased that you've made the effort to learn even just a few words. If you're using your own language, don't just shout loudly! __(5)__ Speak slowly and clearly. And use sign language with a smile, if necessary.

If you want to take a photo of local people, ask them first if it's OK. And don't stare[3] at people. __(6)__ Think about their feelings.

A And if so, how much?
B They're not animals in a zoo!
C But remember, you're a guest.
D Ask them why.
E If people don't understand you, it's not because they're stupid.
F That way, you can be prepared before you travel.
G So don't go round criticizing the country's government.
H People's religion is very important to them.

1	2	3	4	5	6

b Discuss with a partner: Which is the best sentence to end the article? Why?

A The most important thing is: it's *your* holiday, so have a great time!
B All in all, you should be extremely careful not to be a terrible tourist, or people will hate you.
C To sum up, think about other people, be respectful, be friendly and smile!

c Talk to a partner: Where would you like to travel to and why?

SB → p.57

[1] habits Gewohnheiten [2] tip Trinkgeld [3] stare anstarren

9 LISTENING Stories from a tour guide

Listen to a radio interview with Steve, a tour guide. Tick (✓) the correct answers.

> You'll often hear words from more than one answer. Listen carefully to what *exactly* Steve says about them!

1 The majority of tourists ...
- a ☐ cause problems.
- b ☐ are boring.
- c ☐ are nice.
- d ☐ are rich.

2 One American tourist was angry because ...
- a ☐ she didn't meet the Queen.
- b ☐ the tour wasn't interesting.
- c ☐ she didn't like Buckingham Palace.
- d ☐ she couldn't go inside Buckingham Palace.

3 Two young men were ill after they ...
- a ☐ ate bad food in a restaurant.
- b ☐ swam in dirty water.
- c ☐ drank too much.
- d ☐ went to bed too late.

4 A man lost his passport – and found it ...
- a ☐ on the tour bus.
- b ☐ at the airport café.
- c ☐ inside a magazine.
- d ☐ in his hotel room.

5 In Australia, Steve was angry when ...
- a ☐ people didn't listen to his history lesson.
- b ☐ people fell asleep on the tour bus.
- c ☐ people swam in dangerous water.
- d ☐ people didn't respect a place that was special to indigenous people.

6 In Australia, the law says ...
- a ☐ you must wear a helmet if you're cycling.
- b ☐ tourists can't hire bikes.
- c ☐ you must drive on the right.
- d ☐ you mustn't cycle at night.

7 For Steve, the best thing about travelling is ...
- a ☐ the good weather.
- b ☐ seeing how other people live.
- c ☐ trying the local food.
- d ☐ seeing new places.

8 Steve's favourite country to visit is ...
- a ☐ India.
- b ☐ Australia.
- c ☐ Africa.
- d ☐ everywhere!

SB → p.59

10 Useful phrases

a On the Tube, Li Min hears six different people talking. What does each person say next? Find the phrases on the right that follow their sentences on the left and draw lines.

1 You can't stop going on social media, can you! ...	A We're all human.
2 You need a babysitter and I need to earn some money. ...	B It's a win-win situation!
3 My brother has made a website for his band. ...	C You're totally hooked.
4 I don't blame her for making a mistake. ...	D Get over it!
5 So you think my haircut is weird? ...	E Check it out!
6 We need to stop global warming now. ...	F We're heading for disaster!

SB → p.60

b Practice reading the sentences with a partner. Make your intonation good!

11 Li Min has a problem

Read the text and fill the gaps with the correct words from the box. You don't need all the words.

all • by • didn't have • didn't sleep • every • had • hadn't slept • has • have been • if • looking • of • off • since • that • till • though • to • to look • too • was • wasn't having • what • which • while • who • whom • whose

I was really tired yesterday and I told Mum that I ______ well the night before. She already guessed ______ my problem was. She asked me ______ my phone had woken me. In fact, it had woken me up ______ time there was a new message. "You spend ______ much time on your phone!" she said, and I knew that she ______ right. She told me to turn my phone ____ at night. It's a good idea, but I have a friend ______ birthday is today, and I want to see all the photos and comments. Mum says I can wait ______ tomorrow and look then. But it's really hard to stop ______! When Mum was young, she ______ this problem!

SB → p.60

Das kann ich auf Englisch!

Hier kannst du überprüfen, ob und wie gut du alles verstanden hast. Finde auch heraus, wo du dich noch verbessern kannst. Was kannst du schon sehr gut ● oder recht gut ●? Was musst du noch üben ●? Male die Ampellichter entsprechend aus.

1 Ich kann sagen, was unter bestimmten Bedingungen passieren würde.

WB → S.28, Nr.5–6

- Complete the sentences with ideas of your own.

1 If I had enough money, I'd ______________________________.

2 If I lost my mobile, ______________________________.

3 If I met the president of the USA, ______________________________.

4 I'd be very worried if ______________________________.

5 My dad wouldn't be very happy if ______________________________.

2 Ich kann einen Vorgang beschreiben, der in der Vergangenheit begonnen hat und in der Gegenwart noch andauert.

WB → S.29, Nr.7

- Complete the text by writing the verbs in the **present perfect simple** or the **present perfect progressive**.

I ____________________ *(learn)* the guitar since I was 12. My sister also goes to guitar lessons, but she ____________________ *(play)* for eight years – much longer than me! My brother doesn't play an instrument – he ____________________ *(never be)* interested in music. Last week my guitar broke, so this week I ____________________ *(use)* my sister's, which is much better than mine.

Last year I decided to buy a new one, but although I ____________________ *(look)* in shops and online since then, I still ____________________ *(not decide)* which one to buy. My sister ____________________ *(help)* me look, but she's not very good at making decisions either!

FOCUS

The present progressive and simple present

- Verwende das **present progressive** für alles, was gerade im Gang (noch nicht abgeschlossen) ist (z.B. in einem Bild). *The girl is watching TV at the moment.*
- Verwende das **simple present** für alles, was regelmäßig stattfindet (Gewohnheiten, Hobbys, routinemäßige Handlungen) und für Dauerzustände (alles, was immer so ist). *I watch TV every evening.*

You might use these tenses to talk about a picture, then about yourself in the exam.

1 Talking about a picture

Describe what is happening in the picture. Use phrases from the box.

sit beside each other
talk on his phone — not look at the girl
laugh — not smile
not have a good time — maybe: think "..."

____

____

____

____

2 Talking about yourself

a In her English exam, Greta is talking about herself and her family. Underline the signal words / phrases – in pencil for the ones you need the **simple present** for and in pen for the **present progressive**.

b Complete her sentences with the **simple present** or **present progressive**.

I ____________ (use) my mobile phone a lot – I ____________ (post) things on social media, but I ____________ (not write) texts very often. My mum ____________ (not use) her phone much. She ____________ (say) that teenagers ____________ (not talk) to each other enough in real life. At the moment, ____________ (teach) Grandma to use her phone for more things. She ____________ (learn) very quickly and she ____________ (enjoy herself). She ____________ (text) me every day, and she ____________ (go) on social media quite often.

Unit 4 The future - now!

1 Future inventions

a Read this list of some possible kinds of inventions, and write your top four.

something that would ...
- do lots of work, so people would have more free time
- make life safer
- make people more beautiful
- make travel faster
- make cities more beautiful
- make people live longer
- help people who were very ill
- make life more fun
- make people cleverer
- help the environment

My top four inventions would be: something that would ...

b Tell a partner what your top four inventions would be. How many are the same? Give reasons for your choices.

I think an invention that would make life more fun would be great, because I like having fun – and too much stress makes people ill, so people would be healthier.

c Imagine: the government only has enough money to support three projects. Discuss with a different partner which three inventions you think the government should give money for, and why. You can choose inventions from the list in part a) or from your own ideas. SB → p.63

2 Technology: past inventions

a Work with a partner. Fill in section ① of the grid: <u>guess</u> which year the things were invented!

> I think ... was / were probably invented in ...

> No, I think it was a lot earlier / later.

2800 BCE | 100 BCE | 725 | 1286 | 1605 | 1973 | 1810 | 1986

	① Guess the year	② Listen and write the year	③ Listen and write more information
tin cans 			
mobile phones 			
paper 			
mechanical clocks 			
glasses 			
soap 			
driverless cars 			
newspapers 			

b Listen and write the year they were invented in ②. Write some more information in ③.
How many years did you guess correctly?

SB → p.65

3 "People of the forest"

a Skim through the article, and say in one sentence what it is about.

Wild, free, strong and intelligent, orangutans live in the tropical rainforest on the islands of Borneo and Sumatra in Southeast Asia. In fact, the name "orangutan" means "person of the forest" in the Malay language. These beautiful apes are close relatives of humans: we share 96.4% of our DNA with orangutans.

Orangutans spend most of their time in the tall rainforest trees, and even sleep there: every night, they make a new nest of leaves and branches. These nests are complicated, and some orangutans even make roofs or pillows for their nests, yet they can make a nest in only 10–15 minutes. The trees give them most of their food as well – fruit and leaves – and these clever creatures even use large leaves as umbrellas to keep them dry when it rains.

Tragically, the rainforest where orangutans live is being cut down to make space to grow oil palm trees – palm oil is a kind of vegetable oil that is used in all sorts of products from biscuits to toothpaste, so it brings in a lot of money. Over 33 km^2 of rainforest are destroyed *every hour*. This is a real threat to biodiversity in general and orangutans in particular. Experts believe there has been a 55% fall in the number of orangutans in Borneo in the last 10 years and that 80% of their habitat has been destroyed over the last 20 years. Many people believe that to save the orangutan and its rainforest home, companies should use only *sustainable* palm oil – from trees grown on land where there was no rainforest before. There is hope for our long-haired cousins!

b Make a table with the highlighted words from the text. Write the meaning of each word and tick the method(s) you used.

TIP

You can guess some new words. For some, you need a dictionary.

English	German	guess from context	like another English / German word	dictionary
relatives				

c Why are rainforest trees so important to orangutans? Give three reasons.

d What is happening to the orangutan population, and why?

SB → p.67

4 Words in the text

a Find these words in the blurb and the text.

1 a piece of land surrounded by water *(blurb)* – ______

2 a small building that you keep things in, often in a garden *(part 2)* – ______

3 something that helps you find the right direction *(part 5)* – ______

b Find the *opposites* of these words and phrases in the blurb and the text.

1 get lower *(blurb)* – ______

2 stay calm *(blurb)* – ______

3 go faster *(part 1)* – ______

4 huge *(part 1)* – ______

5 hidden *(part 2)* – ______

6 picked up *(part 3)* – ______

7 confidence *(part 4)* – ______

8 forwards *(part 6)* – ______

SB → p.70

5 The 'story' game

In a group of three or four, write a scene in which Zoe finds her parents again.

- Each person has a piece of paper and writes the first line *(see below)*.
- He/she folds it over[1] to hide[2] the line, and gives the paper to the person on his/her left.
- Each person then writes the second line, folds it over and gives it to the next person.
- Do the same for all the lines – then open up the paper and read the stories!

Line 1: Zoe found her parents ... *(how long?)* later.
Line 2: They were ... *(where?)*.
Line 3: Her mum was ... *(doing what?)*.
Line 4: Her dad was ... *(doing what?)*.
Line 5: Zoe said: "..." *(what?)*.
Line 6: They said: "..." *(what?)*.
Line 7: Then they all ... *(did what?)*.

You can make your lines serious, silly or funny!

SB → p.70

6 What do you think?

Write a review for a teen books website (50–60 words), giving your opinion of the story.

- What do you think of the text: the story, the mood and the characters?
- Would you like to read the whole book? Why / why not?
- Would you recommend[3] this book to a friend? Why / why not?
- How many stars would you give the story? (★ → ★★★★★)

SB → p.70

[1] fold over umfalten [2] hide verstecken [3] recommend empfehlen

FOCUS

Adverbs: comparative and superlative

- Einsilbige Adverbien: -er / the -est
  I work quite hard. Holly works harder than me. Amy works the hardest.
- Adverbien mit der Endung -y und andere mehrsilbige Adverbien: more ... / the most ...
  I eat healthily. Rahul eats more healthily than me. Jake eats the most healthily of all.
- Ausnahmen: well / better / the best badly / worse / the worst
- Zwischen Verb und Objekt darf - anders als im Deutschen - kein Adverb stehen: nach dem Vollverb (bzw. dessen Objekt) ist fast immer richtig.
  Wang Yan sings beautifully and she plays the guitar well, too.

7 Mobile phones

Write the right form of the adjectives.

Can you believe it! When Grandpa was young, it was (real) ________ difficult to phone people if they weren't at home, because there were no mobile phones. Now, everyone can phone people a lot (easy) ________________ than before. You can also phone people (cheap) ________________ than when Grandpa was young. Grandpa's new mobile works (good) ____________ than his old one. In fact, his phone works (fast) ____________ than Mum's! My phone works the (fast) ____________ of all, although the battery runs down (quick) ________________ than theirs. It's the (good) ____________ phone, and the (expensive) ________________ of all our phones. And Dad's mobile is the (bad) ____________ of all – it's rubbish!

SB → p.72

8 A strange noise in the house

Make the blue words adverbs and put them in a good place in the sentence.

1 (sudden) Grandpa was sleeping. He opened his eyes. *suddenly* ________________

2 (quick) What was that noise? He picked up his phone. ________________

3 (quiet) He told Mum that there was someone upstairs. He was worried. ________________

4 (careful) He opened the bedroom door. Then he saw the neighbour's cat! ________________

5 (happy) It was washing its face beside the open window. ________________

SB → p.72

FOCUS

Conditional sentences (type III)

- Hiermit sagst du, was *wäre passiert* wenn…
- Das Verb im if-Teil ist im **past perfect**;
  das Verb im anderen Teil ist would (might / could) + Partizip Perfekt.
  If I had known you were fed up, I would have phoned you and we could have gone out.

9 Alice and her mum

Alice and her mum are talking after school. Write the correct forms of the verbs.

"Oh, Alice! If you (be) had ______ more careful, you (not break) ______ that plate and you (not make) ______ a mess on the floor! And you failed your history test at school today – if you (study) ______ harder, you (pass) ______ it. *And* if you (not go) ______ to bed so late last night, you (not fall asleep) ______ in class!" "Well, Mum, if you (want) ______ a perfect child, you (should get) ______ a robot!"

"Oh, I'm sorry, Alice. I've had a bad day, too. Come on, let's make some pancakes."

SB → p.74

10 Alice and her friend

Write the correct forms of the verbs and then match the sentence beginnings with the endings. Write 1–5.

1 If you (tell) had ______ me it was your birthday, …
2 I (visit) ______ you in hospital, …
3 If I (not eat) ______ all my sweets, …
4 We (could go out) ______ last night, …
5 If you (come) ______ to the concert last week, …

___ **a)** if I (know) ______ you were ill.
___ **b)** you (might enjoy) ______ it.
___ **c)** if you (not be) ______ too busy.
1 **d)** I (buy) ______ you a present.
___ **e)** you (could have) ______ some!

SB → p.74

11 LISTENING Taking something back

09

Omar has taken his new drone back to the shop. Listen to the conversation and write short answers.

1 What is the problem?

____

2 When did Omar buy the drone?

____

3 How long does it fly for?

____

4 Why can't Omar exchange the drone?

____

5 So what does Omar ask to do?

____

6 What does the shop assistant suggest?

____

TIP

Remember to change words if necessary, e.g. "*we* don't have ..." → *they* don't have ...

SB → p.75

12 SPEAKING Topic-based talk

Talk about <u>three</u> of the six aspects below. Take 90 seconds to make notes if you wish. Then talk to a partner for about two minutes.

- Don't just say the minimum for each aspect – give details and examples.
- Use phrases to make your talk flow[1] well, e.g. *In my opinion, ... / On the one hand, ... / On the other hand, ... / To sum up, ...*

Technology

- useful technology
- dangers
- future technology
- favourite things
- problems
- price

SB → p.76

[1] flow fließen

13 WRITING A picture story

Verfasse zu den nachfolgenden Bildern eine Geschichte. Gehe dabei auf den Bildinhalt ein und verwende mindestens FÜNF der vorgegebenen Schlüsselwörter.
Du musst nicht alle Bilddetails berücksichtigen.

TIP
Make your story as impressive as you can: use different tenses and verb forms.

★ Schreibe einen Beitrag von ungefähr 150 Wörtern.

Beginne wie folgt:

Mr Brown's new robot
Yesterday morning, Mr Brown was feeling very pleased …

robot • chores • lazy • disaster • break • angry • mess • sorry • promise

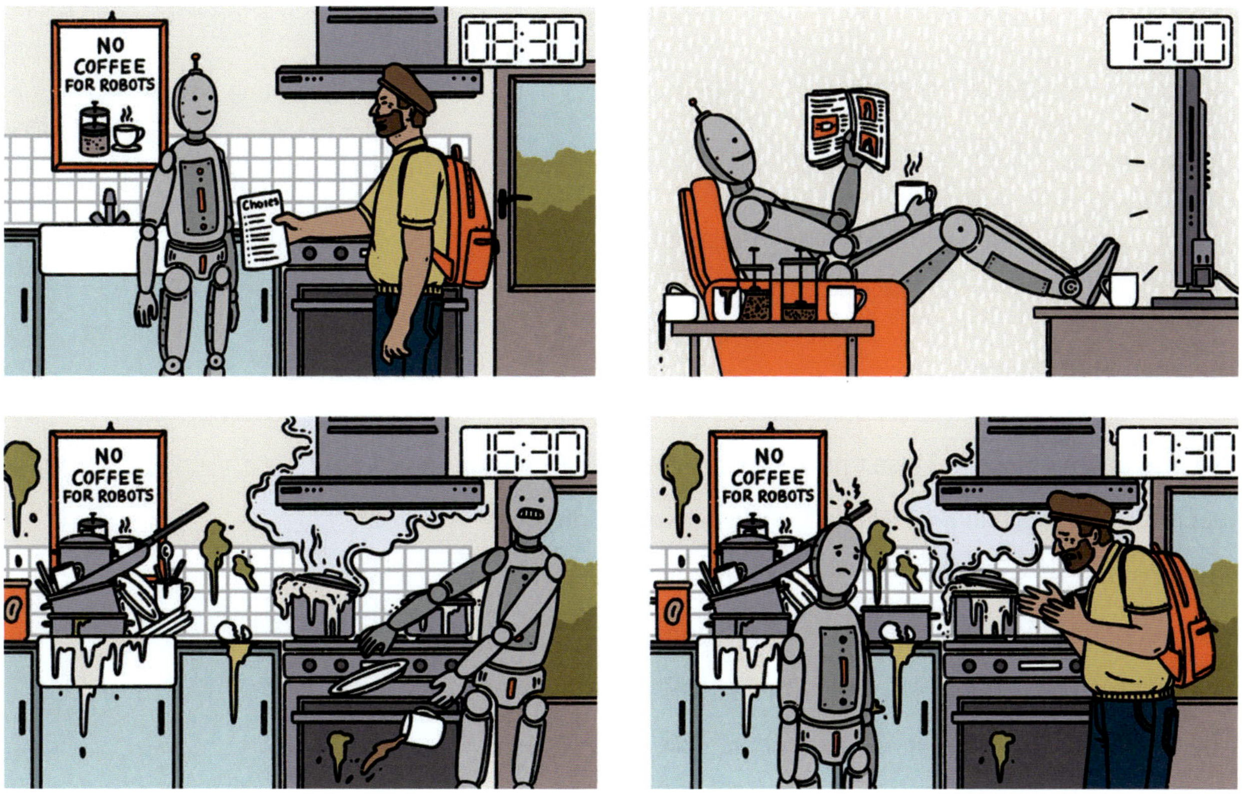

SB → p.77

14 Abbie's dream job

Abbie Smith has written about her job on a teen website. Look at the words in green and write the words from the box in the correct form: *infinitive* (e.g. to go) or *gerund* (e.g. going).

do • dream • find • leave • play • spend • work • write

When I was young, I **used** ______________ all my money on computer games – although I wasn't **allowed** ______________ them in the evening! I was also **good at** ______________ computer programs. I studied hard, especially in ICT. **After** ______________ school, I got a job with a company that produces computer games. I was always **interested in** ______________ work in the industry, and I was so happy to get the job that I had always **wanted** ___________! My advice to young people is that **it's worth** ______________ hard at school. Get the best marks you can in your exams – **it's no use** ______________ of your ideal job if you don't try to get the right qualifications.

SB → p.78

15 The Internet of Things

Find the ten mistakes in the text and write the correct word(s).

The Internet of Things (IoT) isn't new – it's been here since many years. But now it gets bigger. The IoT is the network of physical objects that have specially technology so that they can send informations or receive instructions over the internet. You might have some of these things already – for example a fitness tracker who sends information to your phone about how far you had walked already this week, or a digital assistant that play music if you ask it.

But there are much more that you can do with the IoT. When you're on your way house, for example, you can use your phone to connect to a video camera in your fridge and see what you need to buy. Some people are worry about security, however. Is the IoT in danger from hackers?

1 ______________
2 ______________
3 ______________
4 ______________
5 ______________
6 ______________
7 ______________
8 ______________
9 ______________
10 ______________

SB → p.78

Das kann ich auf Englisch!
Hier kannst du überprüfen, ob und wie gut du alles verstanden hast. Finde auch heraus, wo du dich noch verbessern kannst. Was kannst du schon sehr gut ● oder recht gut ●? Was musst du noch üben ● ? Male die Ampellichter entsprechend aus.

1 Ich kann vergleichen, wie man etwas tut.

- Write the correct form of the word – an adjective or an adverb. WB → S.38, Nr.7–8

Imagine being able to go into town ____________ *(quick)* and ____________ *(easy)* than ever before. You don't have to take your bike and get ____________ *(hot)* and ____________ *(tired)*. You don't have to wait ____________ *(impatient)* for the bus and there's no need to get ____________ *(angry)* looking for somewhere to park.

Electric air taxis are the future, some people say. Old people will be able to travel ____________ *(fast)* and ____________ *(confident)*. However, this method of travelling may be ____________ *(dangerous)* and ____________ *(expensive)* than how we travel today.

2 Ich kann sagen, was passiert wäre, wenn bestimmte Bedingungen erfüllt worden wären.

a Complete the sentences with ideas of your own. WB → S.39, Nr.9–11

1 If my teacher hadn't come to school today, I ____________.

2 If I had gone to a different school, ____________.

3 If it had been −40°C this morning, ____________.

4 I would have come to school by taxi this morning if ____________.

5 I would have called the police this morning if ____________.

b Practise reading the sentences with a partner. Make your intonation good!

FOCUS

Questions

- (Fragewort) – do/does (did / will) – Subjekt – Verb … ?
  Do you work? Where do you work? When did you start there? Will you stay there long?
- *be: Is the bus late? Where is the bus stop? Are there lots of buses?*

You might ask questions in an email, or in mediation (Sprachmittlung) in the exam.

1 An email to a hotel

You are writing an email to a hotel in Plymouth to ask for information. Complete the questions.

New message

Dear Sir or Madam

We are interested in staying in your hotel and have a few questions. (the hotel / have / a lift?)

Does the hotel ____________________? (the rooms / have / wi-fi?)

____________________? We might arrive late. (when / reception / close?)

____________________? (be / a car park?) ____________

____________________ near the hotel, and (how much / it / cost) ____________

____________________ per day? And finally, (at what time / we / have to

check out?) ____________________ in the

morning when we leave?

Thank you for your help.
Yours faithfully

2 Talking to a British girl

On holiday, your sister wants to talk to a British girl, but she doesn't speak good English.
Here are her questions: how would you ask them in English?

1 Wo hast du das tolle T-Shirt gekauft?	____________
2 Was hat es gekostet?	____________
3 Ist der Laden weit von hier?	____________
4 Wann schließt der Laden heute Abend?	____________

12 SPEAKING Picture-based conversation

PARTNER B

a Look at Partner A's pictures. Ask two questions from Set A and three questions from Set B.

Set A
- Describe the differences in the pictures.
- Describe the similarities[1] in the pictures.
- Give a detailed description of what the people are doing in the first picture / second picture.
- What is the general mood of the pictures?
- How are the people in each picture interacting[2] with each other?

Set B
- What are the advantages and disadvantages of camping?
- What are the advantages and disadvantages of staying in a hotel?
- What kind of holiday do you like best and why?
- If you could visit any country, where would you go, and why?
- Who would you most like to go on holiday with, and why?

b Look at the two pictures below for about 30 seconds.
Then answer Partner A's questions. Talk for three minutes.

The environment **Picture 1**

The environment **Picture 2**

Useful phrases

Differences:	Picture A **shows people who** are ...ing.
	On the other hand, picture B **shows** ...
Similarities:	In **both** pictures ...
Mood:	In picture A, people **look** (relaxed / happy, ...)
How they're interacting:	The people are... talking to **each other** / working **together** / ...

SB → p. 21
WB → p. 9

[1] similarity Ähnlichkeit [2] interact aufeinander wirken

1 A holiday in Croatia

You just returned from holiday in Croatia. Here are some messages that you sent your mum while you were there. Now you want to write about your holiday on your blog. Write a short text (about 100 words) about your holiday for your blog.

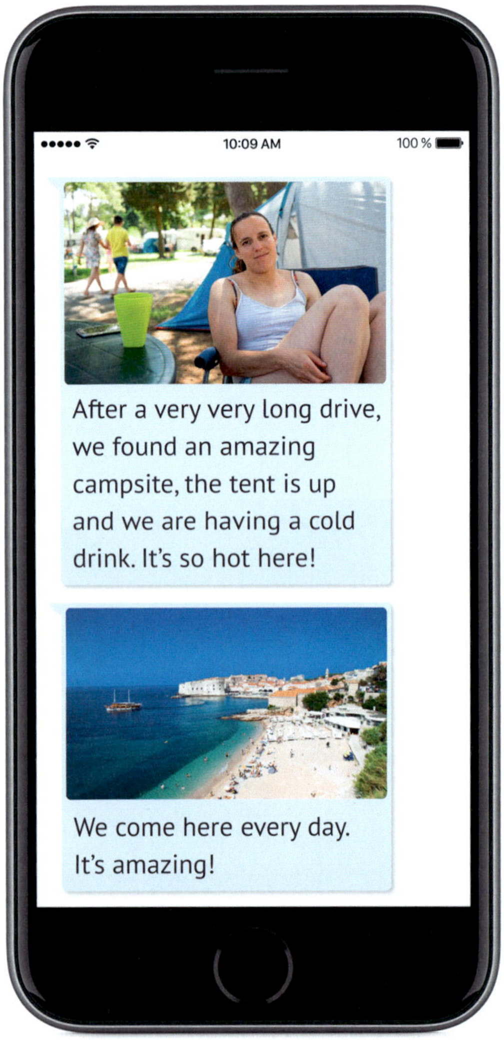

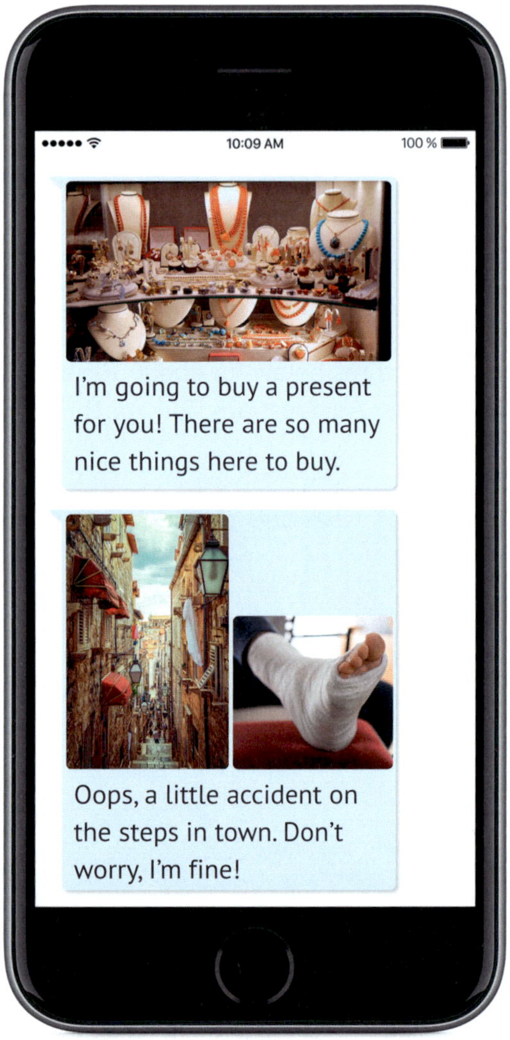

This summer I went ______________________________

____

____

____

____

____

____

EXAM TRAINING: SPEAKING

1 Picture-based conversation

PARTNER A *(Partner B: Go to page 50)*

a Look at the two pictures below for about 30 seconds.
Then answer Partner A's questions. Talk for three minutes.

Shopping in town — Picture 1

Shopping online — Picture 2

b Look at Partner B's pictures on page 50. Ask two questions from Set A and three questions from Set B.

Set A

- Describe the differences in the pictures.
- Describe the similarities in the pictures.
- Give a detailed description of what the people are doing in the first picture / second picture.
- What is the general mood of the pictures?
- How are the people in each picture interacting with each other?

Set B

- What do families often argue about? Why?
- Does the generation gap really exist?
- What sorts of activities do you think are most successful as a family?
- What do you think you will miss most when you leave home?
- Which has the greater influence on young people: home or school?

2 Topic-based talk

PARTNER A

Your topic is *music*. Talk about <u>three</u> of the six aspects below.
You can prepare and make notes if you wish. Talk to Partner B for about two minutes.

music

- favourites
- money
- generations
- technology
- festivals
- performing

1 SPEAKING Picture-based conversation

PARTNER B

a Look at Partner A's pictures on page 49. Ask two questions from Set A and three questions from Set B.

Set A
- Describe the differences in the pictures.
- Describe the similarities in the pictures.
- Give a detailed description of what the people are doing in the first picture / second picture.
- What is the general mood of the pictures?
- How are the people in each picture interacting with each other?

Set B
- What are the advantages of online shopping?
- Do you enjoy shopping in town? Why (not)?
- Do you buy your clothes online or in shops? Why?
- Has the internet in your opinion brought people together or made them more isolated?
- Would you prefer a weekend job in a shop or a call centre? Why?

b Look at the two pictures below for about 30 seconds.
Then answer Partner A's questions. Talk for three minutes.

Family life **Picture 1**

Family life **Picture 2**

2 Topic-based talk

PARTNER B

Your topic is *social media*. Talk about three of the six aspects below.
You can prepare and make notes if you wish. Talk to Partner A for about two minutes.

social media

- advantages
- influencers
- skills
- adverts
- generations
- dangers

1 LISTENING Happy holidays!

Listen to the radio programme. While listening tick (✓) the correct statements.

1 Workers in the USA get
- a ☐ around 20 days holiday per year.
- b ☐ around 28 days holiday per year.
- c ☐ around 40 days holiday per year.
- d ☐ two weeks holiday per year.

2 Many American workers take … of the holidays they are allowed.
- a ☐ 15%
- b ☐ about a quarter
- c ☐ nearly all
- d ☐ about a half

3 A lot of people don't take all their holidays because
- a ☐ they're too busy at work.
- b ☐ they don't like holidays.
- c ☐ they don't have enough money.
- d ☐ their career doesn't allow it.

4 A holiday can
- a ☐ give you more stress.
- b ☐ lead to a new career.
- c ☐ improve your work.
- d ☐ cost people a lot of energy.

5 When they are on holiday, 61% of American workers
- a ☐ switch off their laptop.
- b ☐ work.
- c ☐ have a different job.
- d ☐ don't think about work.

2 LISTENING Having a dog

Listen to part of a radio programme about pets. Fill in the information with a number or 1–3 words.

1 There are about ______________________ dogs and 7.5 million cats in the UK.

2 Having a dog can be good for you. Give two reasons:

a) You ______________________ **b)** You ______________________

3 How does Anne Wilson describe her dog?

It was nice but **a)** ______________________ and **b)** ______________________.

4 Anne Wilson gave her dog to a good home. Why?

Her ____.

12 **3** LISTENING **Do you eat a lot of junk food?**
Listen to the discussion. The teacher, Mr Jones, is asking some students about junk food.

While listening, tick (✓) the name that is the answer to the question.

Who ...	Becca	Molly	Liam
isn't allowed to eat junk food?			
eats a lot of junk food and doesn't worry about it?			
used to eat a lot of junk food as a little child?			
eats less junk food than their parents?			
doesn't actually like junk food?			

13 **4** LISTENING **Living on a houseboat**
Listen to the interview and write the missing information. Use 1–3 words in each gap.

The interviewer is talking with Alice Brown, who lives on a houseboat with (1) ______________ on the River Thames in the centre of London. Alice says that lots of (2) ______________ live on boats near her and she likes the feeling that they're a community. Of course, a houseboat is small inside so you have to be (3) ______________, and you can't have lots of things. She doesn't have (4) ______________. She has given lots of them to a charity shop. Alice says that when she first came to London she started (5) ______________ in the centre of town, but couldn't live there because it was (6) ______________. But she says that there are hidden costs to living on a houseboat. You have to buy fuel for the boat, for example, and you have to buy a boat licence and insurance. And you also have to paint the outside of the boat (7) ______________.

Alice says that living on a boat can be hard work too! There are advantages and disadvantages. But she is very happy living on her boat because every day feels (8) ______________.

1 USE OF ENGLISH **Your own business**

Find the ten mistakes in the text and write the correct words.

Work patterns are changing. Most people are still employing by a company but many people today don't want to have a boss and prefer to work for himself.

Take Murad, for example, who has come to Britain from Turkey in 2017. He learned English very quick and because he was interested at computers he went to college and studied IT.

After college Murad looked after a job but he wasn't able to finding one. So after talking with a friend, Murad decided to start her own business in web design.

"It wasn't easy at the start," Murad told me, "because I not had many customers. First, I didn't have much work, but for three months now I work full time. And I really enjoy it.

Correct word

1 ______________________
2 ______________________
3 ______________________
4 ______________________
5 ______________________
6 ______________________
7 ______________________
8 ______________________
9 ______________________
10 ______________________

2 USE OF ENGLISH **Your own business**

Read the text and write the missing words, using words from the box. There are some extra words in the box.

collected • had collected • have collected • do • doing • done • get • will get • for • had • more influential • most influential • named • were named • were naming • of • to • was • were • when • where • which • while • who • with

In 2013 Melati and Isabel Wijsen, two sisters (1) ______________ live in Indonesia, (2) ______________ swimming in the sea when they suddenly saw an area of water that was full (3) ____________ plastic rubbish. The two sisters were angry (4) ______________ they saw the rubbish and decided that they must (5) ____________ something about it. So they began a campaign (6) ____________ publicize the issue, and they also organized a big clean-up operation in which 20,000 people (7) ____________ 65 tons of rubbish from beaches all around the country.

In 2018 the two girls (8) ____________________________ by Time Magazine as two of the (9) ____________________________ teenagers in the world. Melati and Isabel often talk to young people in schools. "We will only solve the problem," they say, "if young people (10) ____________ involved."

Homeschooling – for and against

Most children go to a school close to their home, while some children live at school and go home in the holidays. But in Britain, unlike Germany, it is legal for children never to go to school and instead be taught by their parents at home. This is known as homeschooling. Why do some parents choose to do this?

1 One reason is that some parents believe that their children will get a better quality of education at home. A child can have one-to-one teaching from a parent instead of being one of up to thirty students in a class, so they can get more help. They can learn at their own speed – they can spend extra time on difficult subjects if they need to, and go quickly through things they find easy.

2 You also don't have to follow an official timetable. Parents can build lessons around the child's own interests, with trips and projects at any time. Children can study things that are not normally taught in school, and do more music or more computer studies, if that is what they're interested in. Lessons can start and end at different times – whatever is best for the family.

3 In addition, some parents think that homeschooling is especially good if their children are very shy, nervous or have suffered bullying at school. These children can learn more easily at home, where there is less stress.

4 On the other hand, homeschooling can have downsides. Homeschooled children usually don't meet so many other young people, so young children may not learn the skills of how to be with other children: sharing, playing, etc. For some very quiet children, having lessons away from other children may make it harder for them to become more confident in their adult life.

5 What's more, most parents haven't had any training to be a teacher, and don't know some of the subjects very well, so their lessons may be much less effective than school lessons – especially for older students. A lot of parents found it very difficult when they had to teach their children at home during the coronavirus pandemic. What is certainly true is that homeschooling means a lot of hard work for home teachers.

6 Another downside is that children miss such school experiences as being in a sports team, choir or school play, going to a prom, a school trip or similar experiences. These are all happy parts of growing up and being at school.

Education is one of the most important things in a young person's life. Whatever parents choose, they must choose carefully!

1 READING Homeschooling

a Match the six correct headings to parts 1-6 in the article. There are two headings that you don't need.

A A safe and comfortable place to learn
B Is homeschooling too expensive?
C Are parents good enough teachers?
D Learning to be with other people
E Choose your own timetable
F Having fun at school
G Children possibly learn better with homeschooling

part of the article	1	2	3	4	5	6
heading						

b Answer the following questions according to the text on page 54. Write short answers.

1 What is homeschooling?

___

2 What difference does the text draw attention to between Britain and Germany?

___

3 Why might some children learn less at home than they would at school?

___

4 What is the result or consequence of homeschooling on the parents?

___

c The following words have more than one meaning. Which is the meaning used in the text? Write the correct number in the box.

1 **close** (line 1)	2 **follow** (line 13)	3 **miss** (line 33)	4 **experience** (line 33)
close[1] *Verb* 1 make something not open 2 bring to an end **close**[2] *Noun* 3 a road with only one entrance **close**[3] *Prep* 4 near ☐	**follow** *Verb* 1 walk behind 2 be a member of 3 respect or live by the rules of sth 4 understand ☐	**miss** *Verb* 1 think (sadly) about a well loved place or people 2 not have the opportunity to do something 3 not go to an arranged meeting or lesson 4 not hit a target (e.g. a goal) ☐	**experience**[1] *Noun* 1 sth that you live through 2 a special event in one's life **experience**[2] *Verb* 3 live through sth 4 suffer (pain) ☐

Three American presidents

A There are two facts that people generally know about **George Washington:** the fact that he was the first president of the USA, and the story about the cherry[1] tree. The story goes like this: when the young George was only six years old, he was given a hatchet[2]. He played with the hatchet in the garden and cut down a cherry tree. His father wasn't happy when he saw the damage and asked George if *he* had cut down the tree. Little George replied, "I cannot tell a lie… I *did* cut it with my hatchet." But instead of being very angry, George's father was extremely pleased – because his son was so honest.

Two well-known facts. **(1).** The story from Washington's childhood was probably invented to show what a good person he was.

B The American War of Independence from Great Britain ended in 1783. George Washington, leader of the army on the American side, was admired for his courage, intelligence and leadership qualities and following the end of the war he was elected president of the newly independent United States. **(2).** His presidency lasted until 1797, and he died two years later.

C **Abraham Lincoln** was the 16th American president. His family wasn't rich and his parents probably couldn't read. **(3)** He had lessons only when travelling teachers were passing near his home, but he loved books and taught himself many things. He used to walk for miles, just to borrow a book to read.

D As an adult, Lincoln went into law and then politics. He was president during the American Civil War, which began in 1861. Lincoln was against slavery, and keeping slaves had become illegal in many states. The Civil War started after eleven southern states, where slavery was still legal, broke away from the United States to become a new country. Lincoln was determined that the USA would stay united, a country where all people would be free from slavery. **(4).** Hundreds of thousands were killed in the war. But Lincoln's side finally won. Lincoln himself didn't live to see peace – near the end of the war, he was shot[3] while at the theatre by John Wilkes Booth, a supporter of the southern states.

E In 1960, **John F Kennedy** became the 35th President of the United States. He was young and glamorous: at 43, he was the youngest president ever. **(5).** He promised better civil rights for African Americans. He talked about fighting poverty, disease and war. But tension with the communist Soviet Union increased, and the USA and Soviet Union came close to nuclear war in 1962. Then, in 1963 the world was shocked when Kennedy was shot and killed.

A man called Lee Harvey Oswald was arrested for the crime, but then he too was shot, and many people today still believe that the identity of Kennedy's real killer or killers is still a mystery.

[1] cherry Kirsche [2] hatchet Beil [3] shot erschossen

2 READING **Three American presidents**

a Which sections match the following descriptions? Write one letter for each description.

	letter
1 In this section, you read that a president was shot, and that some people still ask the question: who *actually* shot him?	
2 This section is about a man being president when Americans were fighting other Americans.	
3 This section tells you about a president who, as a child, was keen to read and learn.	

b Find the time information in the text that corresponds with the notes below.

George Washington became president	following the War of Independence
Death of George Washington	
Presidency of Abraham Lincoln	
Death of Abraham Lincoln	
Death of Lee Harvey Oswald	

c Five sentences are missing in the text. Read the sentences (A-G) and match them with the gaps (1-5) in the text. There are two extra sentences.

A He had very little formal education.
B So he and his wife Jackie were America's golden couple.
C He became known as the "father of his country".
D This was because he was a particularly tall man.
E But only the first is definitely true.
F Nobody had ever had such an idea before.
G So he led the fight to keep the country together.

gap	1	2	3	4	5
sentence					

d Which sentence in the text corresponds to each sentence below?

1 The fighting cost a huge number of lives. *(Section D)*

____

2 He told the black population that they would be treated more fairly. *(Section E)*

____

____

1 MEDIATION **Killer whales**

Dein Neffe interessiert sich für wilde Tiere und ist auf diese Seite im Internet gestoßen. Er hat dich gefragt, was auf der Seite über Schwertwale steht, und zwar über

- Äußere Merkmale
- Alter
- Nahrung
- Sozialverhalten

Notiere die wichtigsten Informationen auf Deutsch (ca. 100 Wörter).

Äußere Merkmale

Alter

Nahrung

Sozialverhalten

Killer Whales

All about killer whales!

1 These black and white creatures are not the largest whales but are maybe the most beautiful, and you might be surprised to know that they are quite like humans in many ways! For example, they live about as long as humans. Like humans too they live all over the planet, from the Arctic to the Antarctic, although not on land of course!

2 Killer whales, also known as orcas, are enormous and can easily weigh from four to six tonnes. They are very social animals, too, and live together in family groups called 'pods'. These are usually led by the oldest female whales, known as 'matriarchs'. Females can have young (called calves) until they reach the age of about 40. Experts believe that these older females teach the younger members of their family everything they need to know to survive.

3 The oldest known killer whale was called "Granny", - she was the matriarch of "J pod", a group of about 25 whales in the northeast Pacific Ocean. She was estimated to have been born around 1911. None of the whale researchers saw Granny after 12th October 2016, so in January 2017 they announced that she had probably died, at an amazing 105 years old.

4 Research has shown that even adult children of these female leaders depend on them. If the mother of a male killer whale over 30 dies, the son is nearly 14 times more likely to die in the following year (only 5.4 times more for a daughter). It is not yet known exactly why this is, but it clearly has importance for the population of killer whales in the wild.

5 What a killer whale eats depends on what it can find. Some only eat fish, others hunt seals and other sea animals. Some people call them the wolves of the sea because they hunt strategically in packs, like wolves.

6 There is no record of wild killer whales ever fatally attacking humans. But surprisingly in many areas killer whales even eat sea birds.

1 WRITING **Express your own ideas**

Answer the question and give three reasons. Write at least 60 words in your exercise book.

What is your idea of a really good holiday?

2 WRITING **An email or a story**

Choose task A or B and write about 150 words.

Task A

Write an email to 'QZ', an online magazine, about an environmental issue in your home area: Say

- what the issue is
- how it began and is developing
- how it affects people
- what has been done, or should be done, to make things better.

OR

Task B

Look at the pictures and write the story in about 150 words. Imagine how the story ends.
Use at least FIVE of the words/phrases below, and begin your story like this: *Last month, Ben…*

invitation • excited • old lady • surprise • wonder • mistake • wrong • feel

Unit 1

1a Drama at the coast

Last weekend, Kara and Ruben *didn't stay* at home – they *went* to the coast. It *was raining* heavily when they arrived, so they *didn't get out* of the car.
While they *were having* lunch, Kara *noticed* a boy in the sea. He *wasn't moving.* They *didn't wait* another minute – Ruben *phoned* the emergency services. While he *was doing* that, Kara *ran* into the sea. When she *brought* the boy out of the water, he *wasn't breathing,* so Ruben *gave* him CPR. Soon, the boy *started* to breathe again. When the ambulance *came,* the boy *was already sitting* in the car.

Unit 2

1 Application for a summer job

I am writing to apply for a summer job at your campsite, where *I stayed* with my parents last April. *We all enjoyed* our holiday with you. Although *I haven't worked* at a campsite before, *I've had* lots of experience of customer service. For example, two years ago *I helped* in my uncle's shop, and last summer *I had* a job at a cafe. *I've been camping* lots of times with my family, so I understand what your customers need.

2 A job application

1 *I've already worked in two clothes shops.*

2 *Last month I did a customer service training course.*

3 *Although I've never visited Liverpool, I've been to the UK five times.*

4 *In my last job, I won 'salesperson of the year'.*

Unit 3

1 Talking about a picture

(example) *The boy and girl are sitting beside each other, but the boy is talking on his phone and he isn't looking at the girl. The boy is laughing but the girl isn't smiling. She isn't having a good time. Maybe she's thinking "I'm bored! / He's very rude!".*

2 Talking about yourself

I *use* my mobile phone a lot – I *post* things on social media, but I *don't write* texts very often. My mum *doesn't use* her phone much. She *says* that teenagers *don't talk* to each other enough in real life. At the moment, *I'm teaching* Grandma to use her phone for more things. She*'s learning* very quickly and she*'s enjoying herself.* She *texts* me every day, and she *goes* on social media quite often.

Unit 4

1 An email to a hotel

We are interested in staying in your hotel and have a few questions. *Does the hotel have a lift? Do the rooms have wi-fi?* We might arrive late. *When does reception close? Is there a car park* near the hotel, and *how much does it cost* per day? And finally, *at what time do/will we have to check out* in the morning when we leave?

2 Talking to a British girl

1 *Where did you buy that great T-shirt?* 2 *How much did it cost?*

3 *Is the shop far from here?* 4 *When will the shop close this evening?*

Exam Training

LISTENING

1 Happy holidays (page 51)

1 *a*; 2 *d*; 3 *a*; 4 *c*; 5 *b*

2 Having a dog (page 51)

1 There are about *8.4 million* dogs and 75 million cats in the UK.

2 **a)** *You get more exercise.* **b)** *You make new friends.*

3 It was nice but *lively* and *noisy*.

4 *Her granddaughter was frightened.*

3 Do you eat a lot of junk food? (page 52)

1 *Liam*; 2 *Molly*; 3 *Becca*; 4 *Liam*; 5 *Becca*

4 Living on a houseboat (page 52)

1 *her boyfriend*; 2 *interesting people*; 3 *really / very tidy*; 4 *lots of clothes*; 5 *a business*; 6 *too expensive*; 7 *every three years*; 8 *like a holiday*

USE OF ENGLISH

1 Your own business (page 53)

1 ~~employing~~ *employed*; 2 ~~himself~~ *themselves*; 3 ~~has come~~ *came*; 4 ~~quick~~ *quickly*; 5 ~~at~~ *in*; 6 ~~after~~ *for*; 7 ~~finding~~ *find*; 8 ~~her~~ *his*; 9 ~~not had~~ *didn't have*; 10 ~~work~~ *have worked / have been working*

2 Cleaning up rubbish (page 53)

1 *who*; 2 *were*; 3 *of*; 4 *when*; 5 *do*; 6 *to*; 7 *collected*; 8 *were named*; 9 *most influential*; 10 *get*

READING

1 Homeschooling (page 55)

a) 1 G; 2 E; 3 A; 4 D; 5 C; 6 F

b) 1 *when children learn at home / from their parents*

2 *Homeschooling is legal in Britain but not in Germany.*

3 *Parents aren't trained / don't know the subjects well*

4 *hard work*

c) 1 close: 4; 2 follow: 3; 3 miss: 2; 4 experience: 2

2 Three American presidents (page 57)

a) 1 E; 2 D; 3 C

b) 1 *following the War of Independence*; 2 *in 1799 / two years after 1797*; 3 *during the Civil War*; 4 *near the end of the Civil War*; 5 *after he was arrested*

c) 1 E; 2 C; 3 A; 4 G; 5 B

d) 1 *Hundreds of thousands were killed in the war.*

2 *He promised better civil rights for African Americans.*

MEDIATION

1 Killer whales (page 58)

1 *schwarz-weiß, sehr schön, riesengroß, wiegen 4–6 Tonnen*

2 *leben ungefähr so lang wie Menschen, der älteste Schwertwal wurde ca. 105 Jahre alt*

3 *Wale essen Fische, Seehunde oder andere Meerestiere.*

4 *sehr sozial, leben in Familiengruppen von ca. 25 Tieren, von den weiblichen geführt; die weiblichen unterrichten die Jungtiere; sollte die Mutter sterben, ist es 14-mal wahrscheinlicher, dass auch die männlichen Kälber früh sterben (5,4-mal wahrscheinlicher als bei den weiblichen)*

Titelbild
Shutterstock.com/Dudarev Mikhail

Illustrationen
Julia Bernhard (**S.8, 10, 13, 19, 25, 33, 35, 39–41, 43, 60**)

Abbildungen
S.4 Shutterstock.com/Tartila; **S.5** Shutterstock.com/Keiti; **S.7** Shutterstock.com/Ingus Kruklitis; **S.9** r. Shutterstock.com/Monkey Business Images, **l.** Shutterstock.com/oliveromg; **S.14** m.l. Shutterstock.com/Lopolo, o.r. Shutterstock.com/Corepics VOF; **S.15** Shutterstock.com/carballo; **S.16** u.r. Shutterstock.com/wavebreakmedia, u.l. Shutterstock.com/Robert Kneschke; **S.17** Shutterstock.com/wavebreakmedia; **S.20** o.r. mauritius images/alamy stock photo/The Photolibrary Wales, u.l. SciencePhotoLibrary/MARTIN BOND; **S.22** Shutterstock/Tap10; **S.27** Shutterstock.com/Vectorium; **S.28** Seretse Kama founding President of Botswana in 1966-1980 here with his wife Ruth Williams arriving in London airport October 20, 1965/Bridgeman Images; **S.29** m.r. Shutterstock.com/Krakenimages.com, u.r. Shutterstock.com/ mdbphoto; **S.30** m.l. Shutterstock.com/ Vibhu Jain, m.r. Shutterstock.com/AlexAnton; **S.31** Shutterstock.com/GoodStudio; **S.32** o.r. Shutterstock.com/Alexey Fedorenko, u.r. Shutterstock.com/Volodymyr Burdiak; **S.34** Shutterstock.com/4contrast_dot_com; **S.36** Shutterstock.com/VH-studio; **S.37** newspaper Shutterstock.com/RTimages, paper Shutterstock.com/Billion Photos, soap Shutterstock.com/Vova Shevchuk, car Shutterstock.com/Scharfsinn, clocks Shutterstock.com/gomolach, tin can Shutterstock.com/Oligo22, glasses Shutterstock.com/Ajintai, mobile phone Shutterstock.com/Erik Svoboda; **S.38** Shutterstock.com/Don Mammoser; **S.42** Shutterstock.com/AnjelikaGr; **S.44** Shutterstock.com/Gorodenkoff; **S.45** Shutterstock.com/Marko Aliaksandr; **S.46** Shutterstock.com/SpicyTruffel; **S.47** r. Shutterstock.com/Andrii Iemelianenko, l. Shutterstock.com/Stella_E; **S.48** Handyrahmen: Shutterstock.com/Alexey Boldin, o.l. Shutterstock.com/Bizi88, m.l Shutterstock.com/Aleksandar Todorovic, o.r. Shutterstock.com/Tupungato, m.r. Shutterstock.com/dnaveh, m. Shutterstock.com/Blue Planet Studio; **S.49** r. Shutterstock.com/VALUA STUDIO, **l.** Shutterstock.com/Iakov Filimonov; **S.50** r. Shutterstock.com/Monkey Business Images, l. Shutterstock.com/David Prado Perucha; **S.51** Shutterstock.com/AnnGaysorn; **S.52** Shutterstock.com/Svetlana Turchenick; **S.53** Shutterstock.com/M-SUR; **S.54** o.r. Shutterstock.com/MNStudio, u.r. Shutterstock.com/Serlena Bessonova; **S.56** o.r. A akg-images/Science Source, m.l. C akg-images/Quagga Media UG, r.u. E akg-images/Universal Images Group/Underwood Archives; **S.59** 1.v.o. Shutterstock.com/Tory Kallman, 2.v.o. Shutterstock.com/Foto 4440; **S.64** Shutterstock.com/Neda Sadreddin.

Unit 2, exercise 8b

Useful phrases for your presentation

Today I'm going to talk to you about ...
Firstly, ... Secondly, ...
One of the things I like best about ... is ...
Another reason I like / enjoy / love ... is ...
... is special because ...
An interesting thing about ... is that ...
Last but not least, ...
To sum up, ...
Thanks very much for listening.
Do you have any questions?